THE WORLD ACCORDING TO THEOLOGYGRAMS

RICH WYLD

DARTON · LONGMAN + TODD

To Ruth, with heartfelt thanks and much love.
Thanks also to Judy Linard, Rob Carson, David Moloney,
Helen Porter, Will Parkes and Ken Ruskin.

First published in Great Britain in 2017 by
Darton, Longman and Todd Ltd
1 Spencer Court
140-142 Wandsworth High Street
London SW18 4JJ

ISBN 978-0-232-53291-3

Designed and phototypeset by Judy Linard
Printed and bound in Turkey by Imak Offset

CONTENTS

INTRODUCTION

The World According to Theologygrams seemed like quite a good title until I came to start work on it, at which point I remembered that I know almost nothing about the world. This was vexing at first, but while it was tempting to try and tell the big story of everything in this book, that doesn't really reflect how I came to theology. Instead, I would say that it began with faith in Jesus, and then I tried to make some sense of it. It turns out that theology has often been thought of this way, as 'faith seeking understanding' (in Latin this is *fides quaerens intellectum*, a phrase that will come in handy in a bit). Because of that, this book is focused quite a bit on Jesus, and is an attempt to make some sense of Christian faith through some badly drawn diagrams.

One of the reasons theology is tricky though, is that we all stand in different places and therefore see things differently. So before we begin, here's a diagram about that. It's based on the work of Hans-Georg Gadamer (1900-2002), a German philosopher who had some helpful things to say about how we understand things from within our own different and changing horizons.

Fido

1. This is Fido. Fido is seeking understanding. Or, as Latin-speaking theologians would say, *Fido quaerens intellectum.*

Tony Williamson

Fido

2. Fido and Tony Williamson see the world from different perspectives, which are limited by their horizons. This makes it hard for them to understand each other.

The giraffe of understanding

3. Fido moves closer to Tony so that their horizons overlap more. But Tony has wandered too, so he now sees the world from a new horizon. What a pickle understanding is!

4. Fido and Tony end up standing in almost the same place. For now they have pretty much managed a 'fusion of horizons'. Well done Fido and Tony! Giraffes are much taller, and so understand everything.

1

IN WHICH THINGS
GET UNDERWAY

This chapter mostly contains diagrams about the Old Testament, and like the Old Testament, begins with some reflections on creation. While I couldn't do justice to such a rich and diverse collection of writings, the Old Testament overall describes the story of the relationship between God and God's people. There are ups and downs, and through it we can learn about God in the midst of the complicated realities of life. We'll also start to look at different ways of making sense of the Bible, and there's a four-headed leopard-creature at one point as well.

BIBLICAL COSMOLOGY

'You stretch out the heavens like a tent' declares the Psalmist (Psalm 104.2). Realistically, I would imagine the writer had something more majestic in mind than this, but it captures something or other of what is suggested. A lot of people have drawn diagrams of how biblical writers thought the universe looked, drawing on passages like Genesis 1, Job 38-41 (which also includes stores of snow and hail), the Psalms, and non-biblical texts from around similar times. This one follows that tradition (sort of), but it's worth remembering that it's not unreasonable to ask how literal these descriptions are meant to be, given that many of them are poetic. By the way, *sheol* refers to the realm of the dead, somewhere underground, and Behemoth and Leviathan, well, err, I think they're probably meant to be scarier.

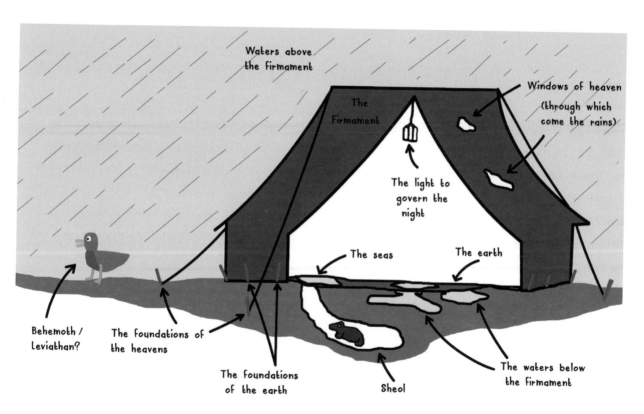

IN THE BEGINNING

'The LORD God formed man from the dust of the ground' (Genesis 2.7). The Old Testament loves puns, and in the Hebrew here, 'man' is *adam* and 'ground' is *adamah*, so the LORD God formed the *adam* from the *adamah*. It's hard to recreate that in English, though some might say that the LORD God created the earthling from the earth. This diagram aims to follow that in highlighting the immediate connection between humanity and the land.

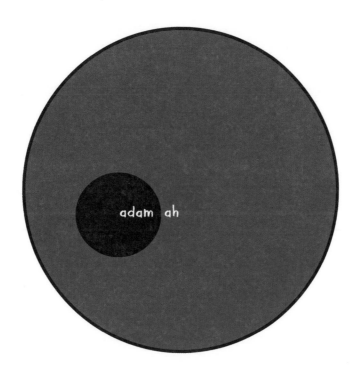

adam ah

SIX OR SEVEN THINGS THE LORD HATES

Skipping ahead slightly, you might have noticed on the previous page that the LORD is written in capitals. Many Bibles do this, and you'd see the same with this bit from Proverbs 6.16-19. Other translations might say 'Yahweh'. When you see either of those, the Old Testament (the Hebrew Bible) has what is sometimes called the *tetragrammaton*, which can be seen illustrated here on a take-away latte cup. The *tetragrammaton* is four Hebrew letters which in English would be YHWH, and have a similar meaning to how God is introduced to Moses in Exodus 3. This might be thought of as God's proper name, and because of that a tradition developed that it was disrespectful in the extreme to say it aloud (for example, in the sentence 'double-shot gingerbread latte for YHWH'). Instead, people would read out the word *adonai*, Hebrew for Lord, and eventually we end up with LORD written in some English Bibles.

I've run out of space to talk about Proverbs though. See overleaf for something about that.

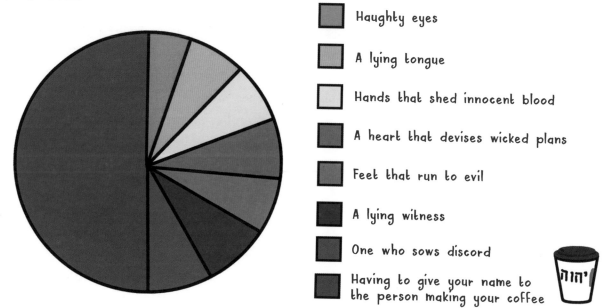

- Haughty eyes
- A lying tongue
- Hands that shed innocent blood
- A heart that devises wicked plans
- Feet that run to evil
- A lying witness
- One who sows discord
- Having to give your name to the person making your coffee

SOME INTERESTING NUMBERS

The bit from Proverbs on the last page is an example of an idiom found in scripture (and beyond), where a point is emphasised by using a number, then adding one to it. It doesn't sound that effective when you describe it like that, but it's worth noticing when the main thing about the numbers is that they're being used expressively rather than literally.

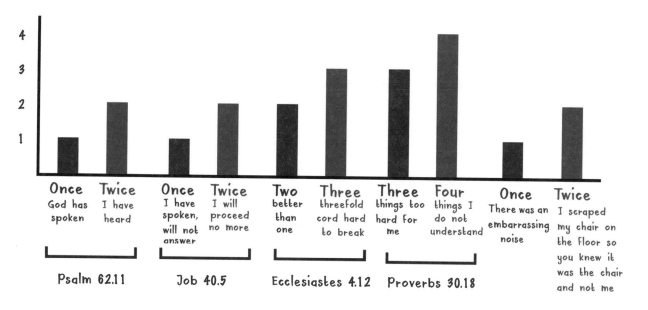

Once God has spoken	**Twice** I have heard	**Once** I have spoken, will not answer	**Twice** I will proceed no more	**Two** better than one	**Three** threefold cord hard to break	**Three** things too hard for me	**Four** things I do not understand	**Once** There was an embarrassing noise	**Twice** I scraped my chair on the floor so you knew it was the chair and not me

Psalm 62.11   Job 40.5   Ecclesiastes 4.12   Proverbs 30.18

THE SECOND COMMANDMENT

Speaking of using numbers for emphasis, that could be what's going on here. A good place to read about the ten commandments is Exodus 20, and the second one is about not making idols or worshipping homemade images.

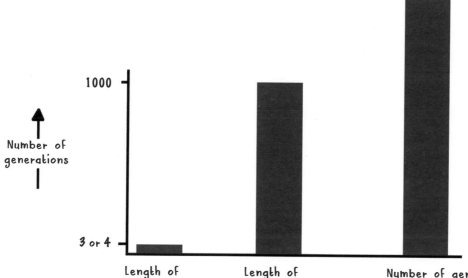

Number of generations

1000

3 or 4

Length of punishment for those rejecting God in favour of idols

Length of steadfast love for those who love God and keep his commandments

Number of generations who complain about how the younger generations have it easy, not like in our day! Forty years we were in that desert I tell you and we never once grumbled, we kept all the commandments like we were told and didn't complain about things when it was hard going ....

19

KEEPING THE COMMANDMENTS

In Deuteronomy 5, Moses calls to mind the drama of when God gave the people (via him) the commandments in Exodus 20. Keeping the commandments turns out to be tricky, so the book of Deuteronomy has the feel of a pep-talk from Moses, before God's people enter the promised land. This diagram represents what some people would describe as an attempt to imaginatively place oneself into the narrative. By some people, I mean me.

The people had been afraid because of ...

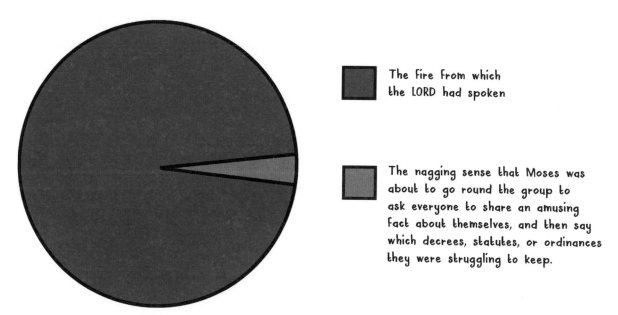

The fire from which
the LORD had spoken

The nagging sense that Moses was
about to go round the group to
ask everyone to share an amusing
fact about themselves, and then say
which decrees, statutes, or ordinances
they were struggling to keep.

GIDEON'S ARMY

You can read about Gideon in the book of Judges, and this incident is in chapter 7. God sends Gideon to battle the Midianites, but also whittles down the size of his army beforehand. The gap between the red and blue lines shows the increasing improbability of victory, making the point that it is not achieved by human might but by God. Gideon's army of 300 rout the Midianites with a fearsome combination of jars, torches and trumpets. If you've ever stayed in a hotel with a Gideon's Bible, you'll see those items depicted on the front.

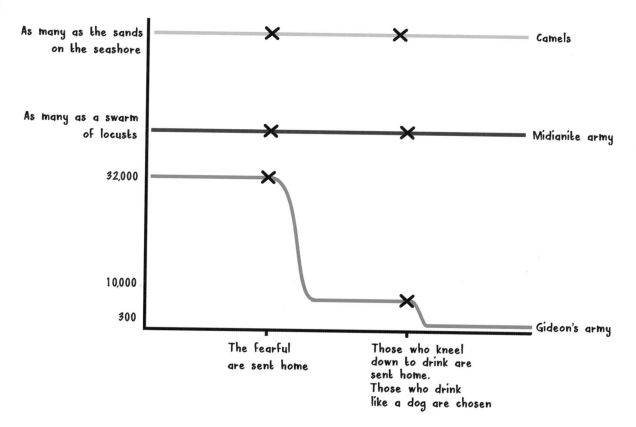

As many as the sands on the seashore — Camels

As many as a swarm of locusts — Midianite army

32,000

10,000

300 — Gideon's army

The fearful are sent home

Those who kneel down to drink are sent home.
Those who drink like a dog are chosen

GOD: ANGER AND LOVE

As well as being generally unimpressed by human might, the Bible also often tells us that God is slow to anger and abounding in steadfast love (e.g., Psalm 103.8). 'Slow' is a bit vague though, so this graph gives it some comparisons.

Unfortunately, these comparisons sort of show why this diagram is a bit silly, because it suggests that God just has a below-average bad temper. But is that really what 'slow to anger' means?

p.s. Psalm 30.5 says that God's anger endures but a moment, so I put in a little downward line at the end.

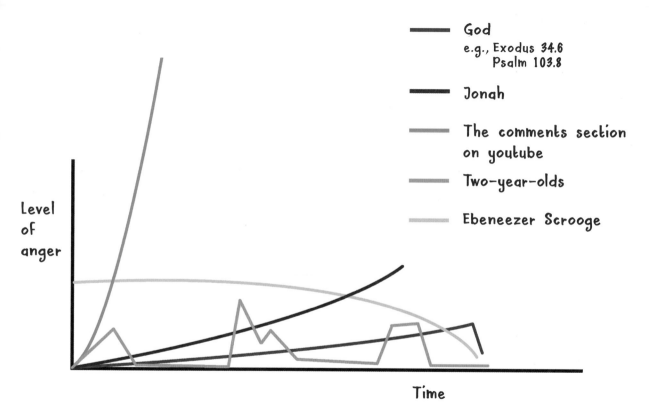

Level
of
anger

Time

God
e.g., Exodus 34.6
        Psalm 103.8

Jonah

The comments section
on youtube

Two-year-olds

Ebeneezer Scrooge

25

GOD'S MOOD-O-METER

If we talk about God being slow to anger, then we could also talk about what kind of mood God might be in. Reading the Bible, you could be led to think that God's mood changes quite radically, as per diagram one. But does that mean God is just another being whose mood is subject to whatever is going on around? By contrast, the Bible (along with a lot of theologians) also describes God as being *unchanging*, unmoved by the fortunes of creation as per diagram two. But does that mean that God is cold and unfeeling towards suffering?

Neither seems quite right; somehow, God is both unchanging and undaunted by the problems of the world, yet responsive to the cries of his people. So diagram three suggests the idea that God surrounds the changes of this world with an unchanging faithful love (*hesed* in Hebrew).

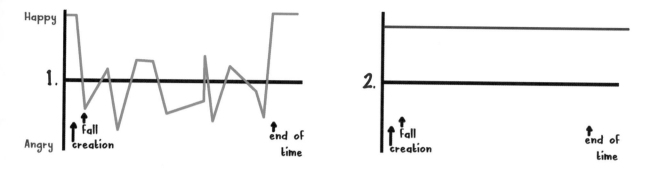

1. Happy — Angry
   Fall | creation ... end of time

2. Fall | creation ... end of time

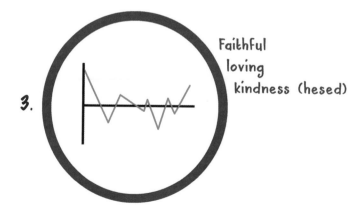

3. Faithful loving kindness (hesed)

PSALM 40.12

'... my iniquities ... are more than the hairs of my head'

Talking about change, the balder I get the more comfort I take from these words. Because I'm definitely not taking them too literally ...

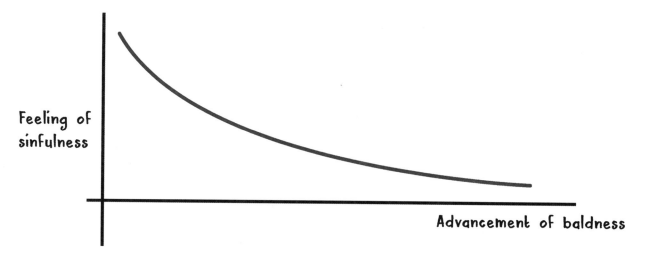

Feeling of sinfulness

Advancement of baldness

TIMELINE OF KINGS

This timeline covers most of the books of Samuel, Kings and Chronicles, from the beginning of the monarchy united under Saul, through the division into the Northern Kingdom of Israel and the Southern Kingdom of Judah, to the exile. It gives a sense of when some of the prophets were active, though it's tricky to pin that down; I've added them in where the texts themselves say they go, but when they were written down is a slightly more complicated question.

I don't know why I did this in the shape of the USB logo. I drew the diagram and it sort of fitted.

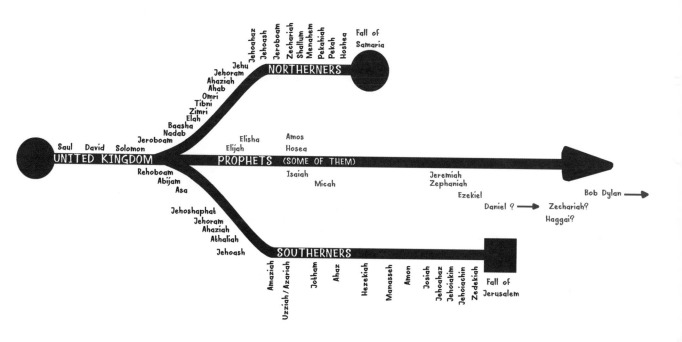

Saul David Solomon

UNITED KINGDOM

NORTHERNERS

Jeroboam
Nadab
Baasha
Elah
Zimri
Tibni
Omri
Ahab
Ahaziah
Jehoram
Jehu

Jehoahaz
Jehoash
Jeroboam
Zechariah
Shallum
Menahem
Pekahiah
Pekah
Hoshea

Fall of Samaria

Rehoboam
Abijam
Asa

PROPHETS   (SOME OF THEM)

Elisha
Elijah

Amos
Hosea

Isaiah

Micah

Jeremiah
Zephaniah

Ezekiel

Daniel ?

Zechariah?
Haggai?

Bob Dylan

Jehoshaphat
Jehoram
Ahaziah
Athaliah
Jehoash

SOUTHERNERS

Amaziah
Uzziah / Azariah
Jotham
Ahaz
Hezekiah
Manasseh
Amon
Josiah
Jehoahaz
Jehoiakim
Jehoiachin
Zedekiah

Fall of Jerusalem

SWORDS AND PLOUGHSHARES

The prophets Isaiah and Micah contain the rather beautiful image of beating swords into ploughshares, expressing the promise of peace and the end of war. Joel then ruins everything by reversing it. Ok, that's not really fair, as the context means that Joel is saying something crucially different. But if we think about what it means to read individual books in the context of the whole of the Bible, then these contrasting images perhaps remind us of the tension of living in a world where things are not yet quite right, but where there is hope. Perhaps today we might say 'they will convert their battleships into cruise ships'. That doesn't quite have the same poetry to it though. Let's move on.

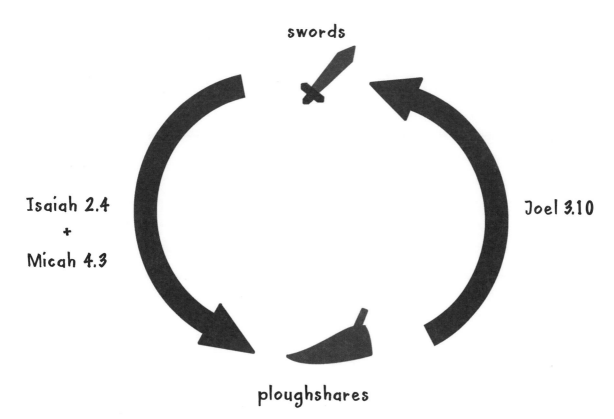

swords

Isaiah 2.4
+
Micah 4.3

Joel 3.10

ploughshares

DANIEL'S FOUR KINGDOMS

Daniel is one of the most visionary, and perhaps difficult, of the larger prophetic books. Future kingdoms are portrayed in vivid images that I have — erm — 'interpreted' for you here. The vision of the statue in chapter 2 seems to tally with the four beasts of chapter 7, but what do these visions represent? The traditional view (arguably going back to Roman times) is column A, but recent scholarship has suggested that Daniel is a much later book written about the persecution of Jewish people under Antiochus IV Epiphanes around 160 years before Jesus. If that's right, column B makes more sense. As well as thinking about how these texts work, perhaps the uncertainty reminds us that even if we don't know the exact historical backdrop, the texts can still meaningfully be read. And also, four-headed leopards.

Daniel 2.31-45
Nebuchadnezzar's dream

Daniel 7.1-28
Daniel's dream / vision

Corresponding
Kingdoms / Empires

A	B
Babylonian	Babylonian
Medo-Persian	Median
Greek	Persian
Roman	Greek

THE MINOR PROPHETS

Micah and Joel, who appeared a few pages back, are part of a collection of twelve shorter prophetic books. The twelve range around the questions of faithfulness to God, warnings of coming judgement, and promises of restoration. But they are also quite varied, through the narrative of Jonah, the visions of Zechariah, and the brevity of Obadiah. This chart offers a sense of their similarities and differences.

HOSEA

JOEL

AMOS

OBADIAH

JONAH

MICAH

NAHUM

HABAKKUK

ZEPHANIAH

HAGGAI

ZECHARIAH

MALACHI

JUDGEMENTS

= imminent destruction

= critique of injustice

= critique of idolatry

= judgement over the nations

HOPES

= hope for God's people

= day of the LORD

= hope for the nations

IMAGES + VISIONS

= bad weather

= trumpets

= aquatic creatures

= lions

= locusts

= horses

= put on sackcloth

37

2

IN WHICH JESUS IS INTRODUCED

I couldn't quite decide how to arrange this book, but it did occur to me that while I think the message of Jesus is for everyone, he nonetheless teaches and does things in a particular time and place. To understand what Jesus is about it can be helpful to understand the world into which he came, so this chapter looks a bit into the background to what we are told about Jesus himself. Some of the diagrams here look at connections between the Old Testament and Jesus, some look at how the Gospels go about telling his story, and some describe the context in which he lived. And there's one about the hymn Silent Night.

MATTHEW'S GENEALOGY OF JESUS

Matthew — and therefore the whole New Testament — begins with a genealogy that takes us from Abraham to Jesus. And if it's good enough for Matthew then it's good enough for this chapter. But I suspect this seems like a very odd way to start a book to many of us, and perhaps we are tempted to skip over it. So why would Matthew do this? It might partly be to show off Jesus's royal heritage, and make a bold statement about who Jesus is from the start. But what this diagram also does is to explore how a list of names can actually tell a story by calling to mind what all those people did, and when. So this genealogy also suggests that Jesus is the culmination of the history of God's people. And that's quite a big opener.

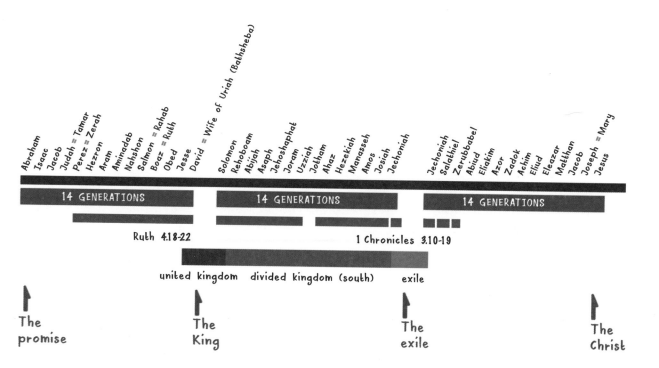

Abraham
Isaac
Jacob
Judah = Tamar
Perez = Zerah
Hezron
Aram
Aminadab
Nahshon
Salmon = Rahab
Boaz = Ruth
Obed
Jesse
David = Wife of Uriah (Bathsheba)

Solomon
Rehoboam
Abijah
Asaph
Jehoshaphat
Joram
Uzziah
Jotham
Ahaz
Hezekiah
Manasseh
Amos
Josiah
Jechoniah

Jechoniah
Salathiel
Zerubbabel
Abiud
Eliakim
Azor
Zadok
Achim
Eliud
Eleazar
Matthan
Jacob
Joseph = Mary
Jesus

14 GENERATIONS
14 GENERATIONS
14 GENERATIONS

Ruth 4:18-22
1 Chronicles 3:10-19

united kingdom   divided kingdom (south)   exile

The
promise

The
King

The
exile

The
Christ

JOHN'S PROLOGUE (1)

Whereas poor Matthew's genealogy gets ignored quite often, John's opener is an absolute belter, and gets read at least every Christmas. It is a rich passage; Jesus is the word of God, the logic of the universe and God's ultimate revelation to humankind. But there are also parallels between what is said about Jesus and what is said about wisdom in some of the wisdom books of the Old Testament and beyond. Yet all these ideas are grounded (sort of literally) in the coming of Christ in real human flesh, the event generally called the Incarnation.

Bearing all that in mind, I've left a lot of this diagram blank as I suspect filling bits of it in would lead me off into some dangerously heretical territory.

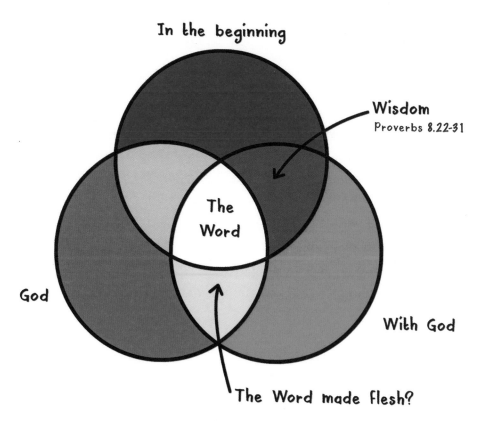

In the beginning

Wisdom
Proverbs 8.22-31

The
Word

God

With God

The Word made flesh?

43

JOHN'S PROLOGUE (2)

This diagram basically describes what creation consists of, according to my own interpretation of John chapter 1. There is an echo (though not a repetition) here of what is said about wisdom and creation in Proverbs 8. And, compare it to Colossians 1.16.

p.s. This diagram is definitely wrong, as John says *all* things are made through the word. But sometimes you have to look harder to see the hand of God, not least when you're trying to eat anything with jam whilst dining *al fresco*.

Creation consists of ...

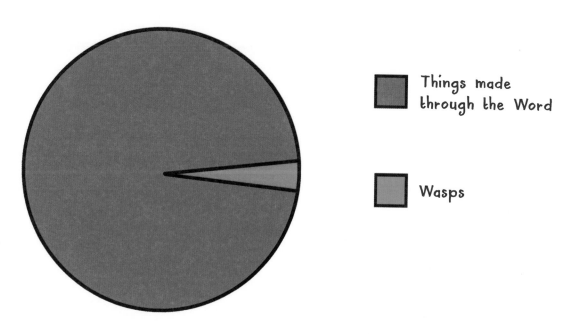

Things made
through the Word

Wasps

PROPHECY AND FULFILMENT

As part of the nativity, Matthew tells the story of an indeterminate number of wise men who bring gold, frankincense, and myrrh to Jesus. While Matthew doesn't make an explicit reference to it, the story is often linked to Isaiah 60 which describes gifts of gold and frankincense, but also a multitude of camels. I think the link is important, but the differences shown here also make us think about what the gospel writers really mean by fulfilling the Old Testament scriptures. So for example, Jesus's parents don't feel the need to find camels and flog the myrrh as quickly as possible, just to prove that Isaiah predicted it 100% right. I think the idea of fulfilment is much subtler than that, and the differences can be as instructive as the similarities.

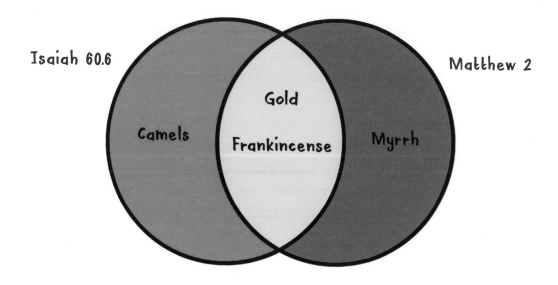

Isaiah 60.6

Matthew 2

Camels

Gold
Frankincense

Myrrh

ISAIAH 9.7

'... of the increase of his government and of peace there shall be no end' (KJV)

This is another text from Isaiah that is often connected to Jesus. It's meant to be a three-dimensional graph and so I wanted to make it into a pop-up section. But we couldn't afford that.

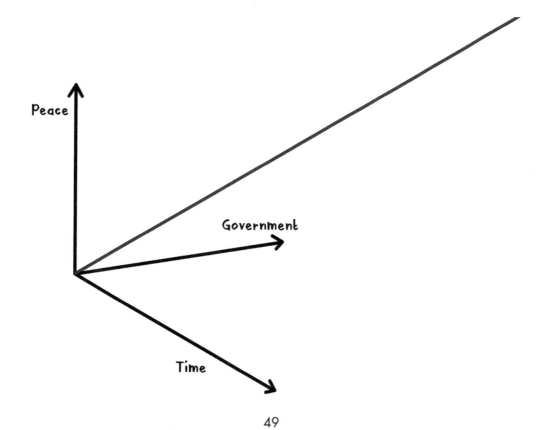

Peace

Government

Time

THE KINGDOM OF GOD

When Jesus begins preaching, his message is simply that the Kingdom of God (or Heaven in Matthew's gospel) is close at hand. At other times, the Kingdom is suggested to be much closer. This is often recognized as a deliberate tension between the Kingdom having arrived in Jesus, and the Kingdom still being yet to come. This might be less of a problem if we think about the kingdom being not so much an earthly kingdom or realm, but rather think of it as referring to the reality of God being in charge and putting the world right.

Your current location
(in time?)

The kingdom of
God/Heaven

THE LEVITICAL PROPERTY LADDER

In another early bit of Jesus's preaching he quotes Isaiah to announce, among other things, the arrival of the year of the Lord's favour (Luke 4.19). This is often thought to refer us back to the book of Leviticus (chapter 25), which sets out the idea that every 49 or 50 years (after seven sevens of years), there is a jubilee year where debts are cancelled, people are set free and the land rests. It's not clear to what extent this law was practised, and Jesus is perhaps speaking more about the broader principle than he is about obeying this law to the letter. But either way the idea seems central to his message.

In passing, I drew the little person who has just relinquished a lot of property as being very happy about it. This seems counterintuitive, but I do think the idea of jubilee is supposed to be good news for everybody, rich and poor alike.

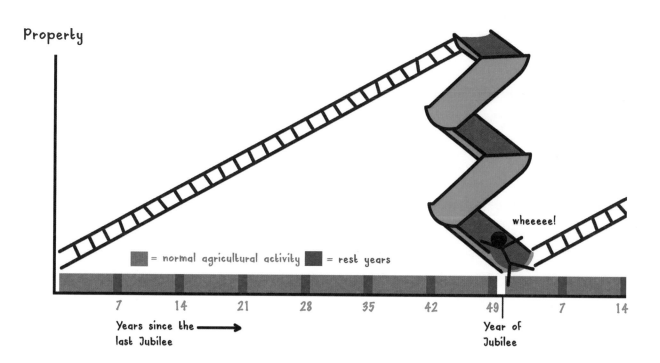

Property

= normal agricultural activity | = rest years

wheeeee!

7 14 21 28 35 42 49 7 14

Years since the ⟶ last Jubilee

Year of Jubilee

53

VARIOUS SECTS FROM THE TIME OF JESUS

The Jewish historian Josephus (writing in the 1st century) describes at least three main religious groups around the time of Jesus. This description might explain why Jesus clashed most with the Pharisees; the Sadducees were less present among the people, and the Essenes were either in the wilderness or just keeping themselves to themselves. Although there are important differences, there are also interesting similarities. What does Jesus also have in common with the Pharisees? Had John the Baptist once been an Essene? I'll leave that to you, and I've also left some of the bottom line open, because I think it's not totally straightforward — I've added some thoughts about Jesus and the law on page 92.

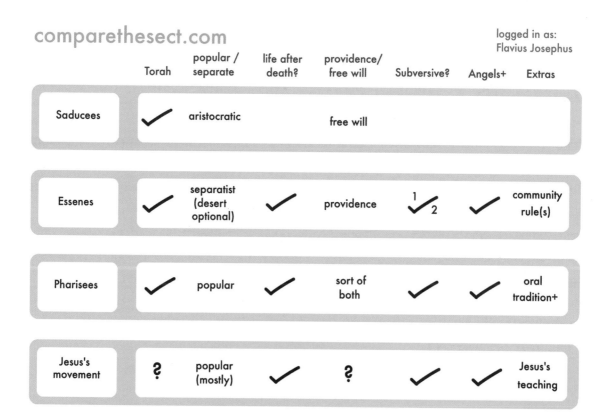

comparethesect.com

	Torah	popular / separate	life after death?	providence/ free will	Subversive?	Angels+	Extras
Saducees	✔	aristocratic		free will			
Essenes	✔	separatist (desert optional)	✔	providence	1 ✔ 2	✔	community rule(s)
Pharisees	✔	popular	✔	sort of both	✔	✔	oral tradition+
Jesus's movement	?	popular (mostly)	✔	?	✔	✔	Jesus's teaching

A MAP OF GALILEE

Here is a map of Galilee, with some words describing what happened where. I haven't put any references in to the relevant passages, so there's a fun challenge for you.

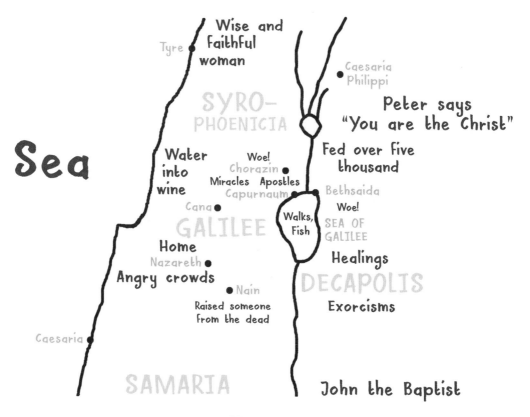

Sea

Tyre

Wise and Faithful woman

SYRO-PHOENICIA

Caesaria Philippi

Peter says "You are the Christ"

Water into wine

Woe!
Chorazin

Miracles Apostles
Capurnaum

Fed over five thousand

Bethsaida
Woe!

SEA OF GALILEE

Cana

GALILEE

Walks, Fish

Home
Nazareth

Healings

Angry crowds

DECAPOLIS

Nain

Raised someone from the dead

Exorcisms

Caesaria

SAMARIA

John the Baptist

PUNCTUATION IN ISAIAH

I'm not 100% sure if this counts as a diagram, but there is an arrow, so that's something. While John (the gospel writer) phrases it slightly differently, all the gospels describe John the Baptist's work in preparing the way for Jesus as a fulfilment of Isaiah 40. Because John is in the wilderness, it makes sense that the gospels talk about a voice crying out in the wilderness. But (without going into the history of biblical punctuation), Isaiah was generally read as meaning that the way of the Lord should be prepared in the wilderness, rather than that the voice was crying out in the wilderness. Well, hopefully this diagram makes the point clearer.

Did something go wrong in translation? Maybe. But then we should ask why John was in the wilderness in the first place. Is John responding to the prompting of Isaiah? More importantly, what does the wilderness symbolize so that it matters that the good news is proclaimed there?

Isaiah 40.3

A voice cries out: 'In the wilderness prepare the way of the LORD'

A voice cries out in the wilderness: 'Prepare the way of the LORD'

Matthew 3.3 // Mark 1.3 // Luke 3.4 // John 1.23

JESUS'S APOSTLES: MATTHEW'S STARTING LINE-UP

For some reason, thinking about this always makes me feel guilty for not knowing more about Thaddaeus.

1. Known as 'The Rock'

2. Known as 'The Sons of Thunder' (Mark 3)
   asked to play left and right (Mark 10.37)

3. son of Alphaeus

Mark and Luke switch
Thomas and Matthew

4. a.k.a. Lebbaeus in some manuscripts
   Luke plays Judas son of James
   in this position

5. called the Canaanean (Matthew and
   Mark) or the Zealot (Luke)

6. Luke substitutes Matthias in
   the second half

7. There's probably a joke about Jesus
   being in goal

JOHN'S GOSPEL

John's story of Jesus is well crafted, and people often draw out groupings of seven, which was a number representing wholeness. Although most of what happens up to chapter 12 is in narrative from, while most of what happens from chapter 13 up to the passion is Jesus speaking, you can begin to see how those two big sections are still drawn together.

Some of the festivals mentioned give context to Jesus's words; the bread of life is connected with Passover, and the light of the world is possibly connected with the feast of tabernacles which included large torches in the temple and in special processions.

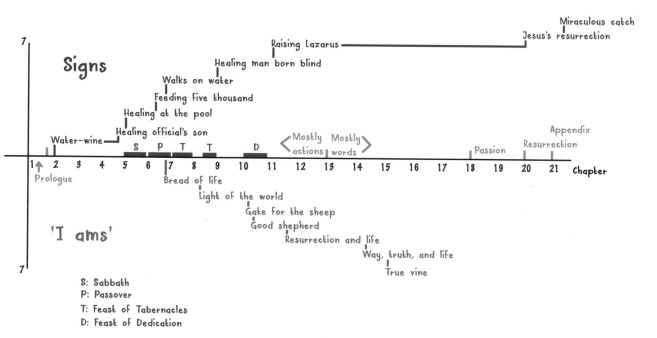

Signs

Miraculous catch
Jesus's resurrection
Raising Lazarus
Healing man born blind
Walks on water
Feeding five thousand
Healing at the pool
Healing official's son
Water-wine

⟨ Mostly   Mostly ⟩
actions   words

Appendix
Resurrection
Passion

1 2 3 4 5 6 7 8 9 10 11 12 13 14 15 16 17 18 19 20 21   Chapter
         S   P T T   D

Prologue

Bread of life
Light of the world
Gate for the sheep
Good shepherd
Resurrection and life
Way, truth, and life
True vine

'I ams'

7

S: Sabbath
P: Passover
T: Feast of Tabernacles
D: Feast of Dedication

THE NATIONAL TRUST GUIDE TO THE TEMPLE OF JESUS'S DAY

Take this with a pinch of salt.

The Temple in Jesus's Day

→N

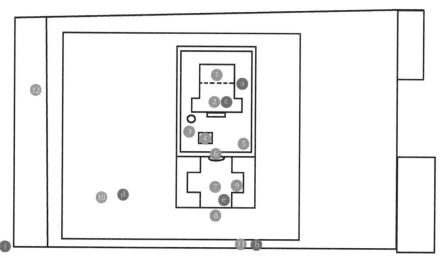

(a) Temple curtain. Damaged early-mid 1st Century. (Matthew 27.51)

(b) Walking route (John 10.23)

(c) Restricted access (Luke 1.9-11)

(d) Entry and gift shop (Matthew 21.12-14)

(e) Donations and gift aid (Luke 21.1-4)

(f) Pinnacle? (Matthew 4.5)

1. Holy of Holies
2. Sanctuary + incense altar
3. Laver / table?
4. Altar
5. Court of Priests
6. Nicanor's Gate
7. Court of Women
8. Beautiful Gate
9. Treasury
10. Court of Gentiles
11. Solomon's Portico
12. Royal Portico

THE FOUR GOSPELS

Each of the four gospels has its own individual flavour, and so all four build up a much richer testimony to Jesus than just one could. From as early as Irenaeus (writing around the 2nd Century AD), some commentators have represented the different flavours of the gospels by drawing on the four animal faces of the heavenly beings described in Ezekiel 1, which are then picked up differently in Revelation 4. At various times the different faces have been connected differently to the gospels, but the formation shown here is fairly common following St. Jerome (d. AD 420), who translated most of the Bible into Latin.

To be fair, I don't know why I took this on. They're supposed to be a human, a lion, an ox and an eagle respectively. John looks more like a seagull, Luke like a Moomin, and who knows what's going on with Mark.

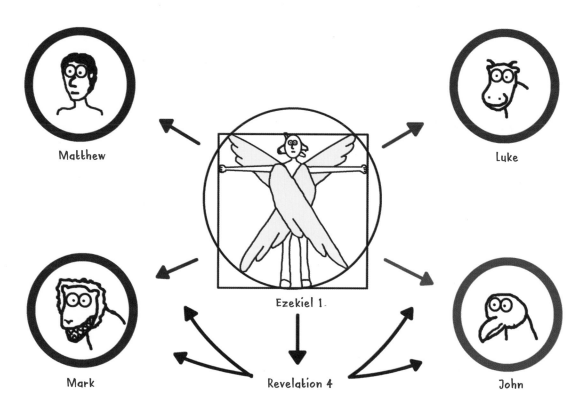

Matthew

Luke

Ezekiel 1

Mark

Revelation 4

John

SILENT NIGHT

I'm also not sure why I did this.

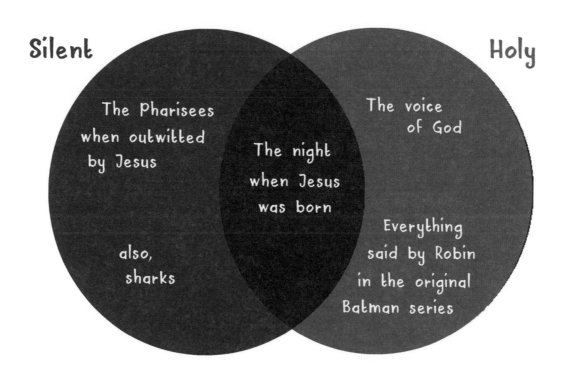

Silent

Holy

The Pharisees when outwitted by Jesus

also, sharks

The night when Jesus was born

The voice of God

Everything said by Robin in the original Batman series

3

IN WHICH JESUS PROCLAIMS SOME GOOD NEWS

OK, *the* good news, but we're going to look more broadly at some of Jesus's teaching and actions, and how they build up a picture of what Jesus means to the world. Obviously that makes it sound like this is a very in-depth exploration, and I don't want you to get your expectations up. At best, I hope the visual representation helps to consider what Jesus says in a new way. Yep, we'll go with that for now.

THE BEATITUDES

'The Beatitudes' are a quite profound part of an already profound body of teaching that we usually call the Sermon on the Mount (Matthew 5-7). Luke records a partially similar body of teaching generally referred to as the Sermon on the Plain (Luke 6), which also has some beatitudes. You can see here that some are shared between Matthew and Luke, while two that are more spiritual in tone for Matthew echo two that are more physical in Luke. So does Matthew spiritualize Luke's version, or does Luke politicize Matthew's? Or, as I like to think, did Jesus give a whole range of sermons that sometimes varied in content depending on the circumstances?

Either way, I think both together offer food for thought, not least when we consider how we use the language of being blessed (or happy in some translations) today.

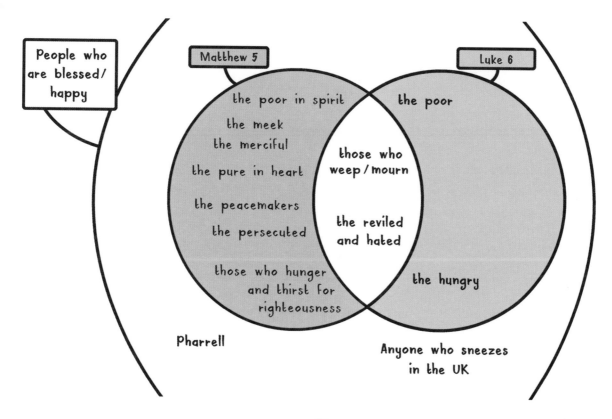

People who are blessed/ happy

Matthew 5

Luke 6

the poor in spirit

the meek
the merciful

the pure in heart

the peacemakers
the persecuted

those who hunger and thirst for righteousness

those who weep/mourn

the reviled and hated

the poor

the hungry

Pharrell

Anyone who sneezes in the UK

THE LIGHT OF THE WORLD

Here is another section of the Sermon on the Mount (Matthew 5.14-16). Notice that in John's Gospel Jesus describes himself as the light of the world. Here it is Jesus's listeners who are the light of the world.

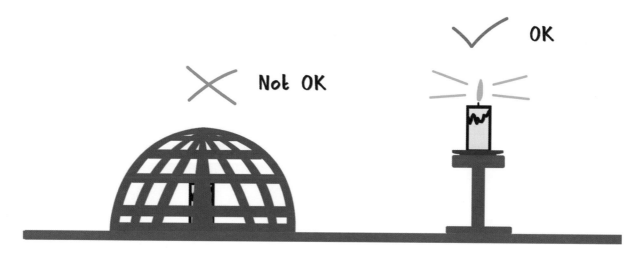

Not OK

OK

CONSIDER THE LILIES

In Matthew 6.25-end, Jesus goes on to tell us not to worry, which is advice we've all given but has probably never worked. Except that I don't think Jesus is serving up trite 'be-platitudes'. Get it? Sorry.

Anyway, this passage has less to do with telling those who are genuinely struggling to get by not to worry, and more to do with presenting two visions of the world; one involves pursuing material wealth, the other in pursuing the kingdom of God.

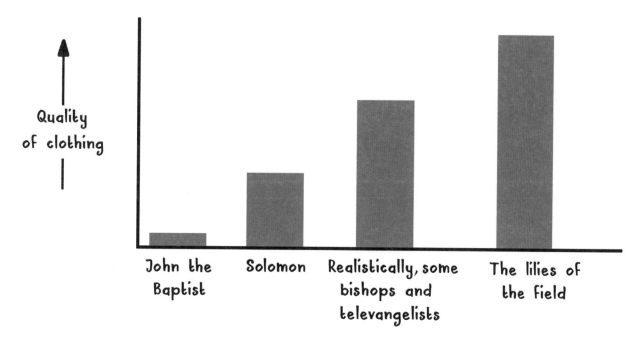

RAIN

In teaching people to love their enemy, Jesus describes how God does not distinguish between the good and the bad in bestowing goodness. The analogy works well, though clearly some people might feel that they've got the rough end of that deal.

People on whom God makes it rain ...
(Matthew 5.45)

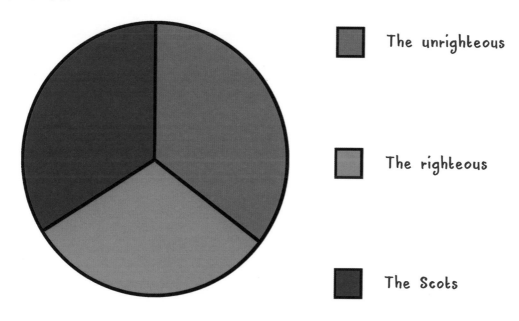

The unrighteous

The righteous

The Scots

JESUS CALMS THE STORM

Having power over the elements is a particularly significant divine attribute. In the Bible that is. It calls to mind God creating harmony in the Genesis story of creation. Jonah on the other hand really just gets chucked overboard and ends up inside a fish. That calmed the storm, but it was a pretty tough call for Jonah.

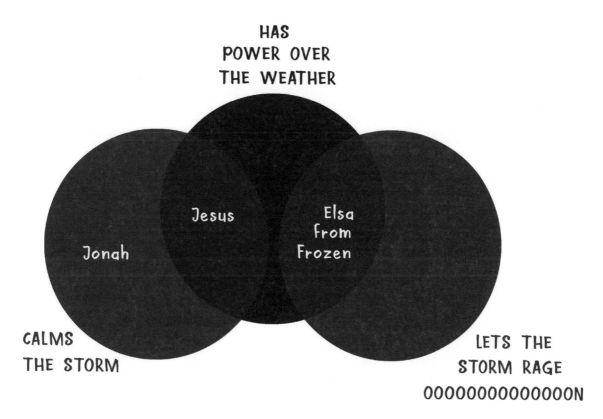

HAS
POWER OVER
THE WEATHER

Jonah

Jesus

Elsa
from
Frozen

CALMS
THE STORM

LETS THE
STORM RAGE
OOOOOOOOOOOOOOON

NARRATIVE INTERPOLATIONS

There's something very satisfyingly clever sounding about the phrase 'narrative interpolations'. Not that I'm claiming to have come up with it. What it refers to is the way that some of the gospels use a technique of sandwiching a small story inside another story. The mini-story inside sheds light on the story it sits within. Another less immediate example in Mark would be the execution of John sandwiched between the sending out and returning of the disciples (Mark 6.7-31), or fig tree and the temple (Mark 11.21-25).

Oh, and Fido has returned. 'Breakfast' may not seem like much of a story as such, though I think it probably is to a dog. But noting the symmetry, Fido's morning routine could also be described as a chiasm, on which see page 114.

a. Mark 5.21-43

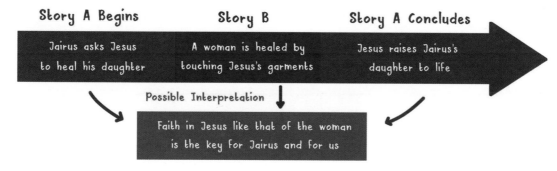

Story A Begins

Jairus asks Jesus to heal his daughter

Story B

A woman is healed by touching Jesus's garments

Story A Concludes

Jesus raises Jairus's daughter to life

Possible Interpretation

Faith in Jesus like that of the woman is the key for Jairus and for us

b. Literally every morning

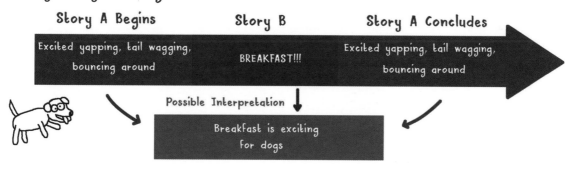

Story A Begins

Excited yapping, tail wagging, bouncing around

Story B

BREAKFAST!!!

Story A Concludes

Excited yapping, tail wagging, bouncing around

Possible Interpretation

Breakfast is exciting for dogs

JESUS SENDS OUT HIS DISCIPLES

On the previous page I mentioned how Mark narrates the story of John's execution in the middle of the story about Jesus sending the disciples out. Telling the story like that serves as a reminder of the challenges that the discples, like many followers of Jesus, will face. That's kind of the mood here as well, from Matthew 10.16.

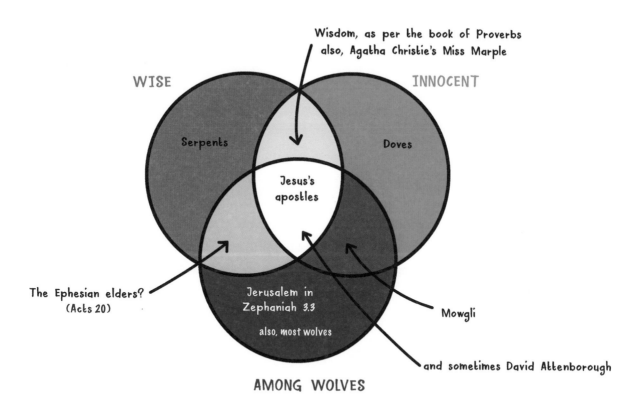

WISE

INNOCENT

Wisdom, as per the book of Proverbs
also, Agatha Christie's Miss Marple

Serpents

Doves

Jesus's
apostles

The Ephesian elders?
(Acts 20)

Jerusalem in
Zephaniah 3:3

also, most wolves

Mowgli

and sometimes David Attenborough

AMONG WOLVES

THE PARABLE OF THE WORKERS

Matthew 20.1-16

This parable suggests that the reward of the kingdom of heaven is not based on how deserving we might think we are, but on God's graciousness. For those who felt themselves unworthy, this is very good news. For those who felt themselves worthy, like those who were hired at the start of the day (and a bit like the older son in the parable of the prodigal son in Luke 15), this is still good news, but it might take a bit of an adjustment to take that on board. And perhaps alongside the spiritual dimension to this, there's a dig at the economic situation in which many people couldn't find enough work to survive on. By contrast to that, Jesus describes a situation where everyone's needs are met, rather than left to luck.

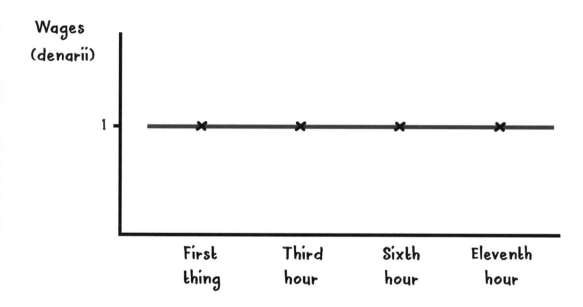

CASTING THE FIRST STONE

John 8 tells the story of Jesus challenging the Scribes and Pharisees who were about to stone a woman, by telling them that if any of them is without sin, they can cast the first stone. They all know they are sinners too, so walk away one by one. It's a challenge that is so effective that the words 'cast the first stone' are still quite widely known, whether or not people know where they come from. After Jesus has laid down his challenge, he writes in the sand while the Scribes and Pharisees slowly walk away. What did Jesus write? There are numerous suggestions. Here is mine.

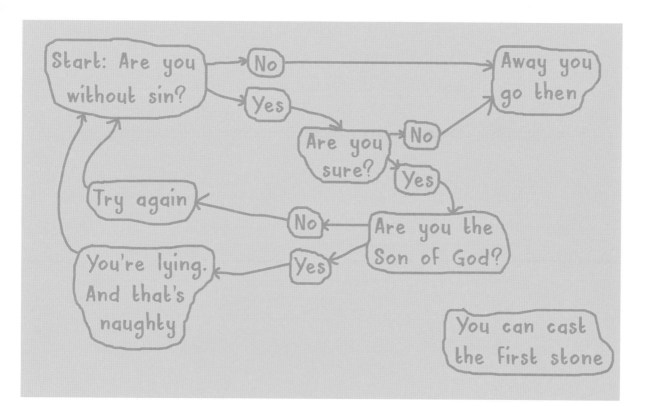

BIBLICAL VILLAINY

To be fair, a fancy costume on its own probably doesn't make you a villain.

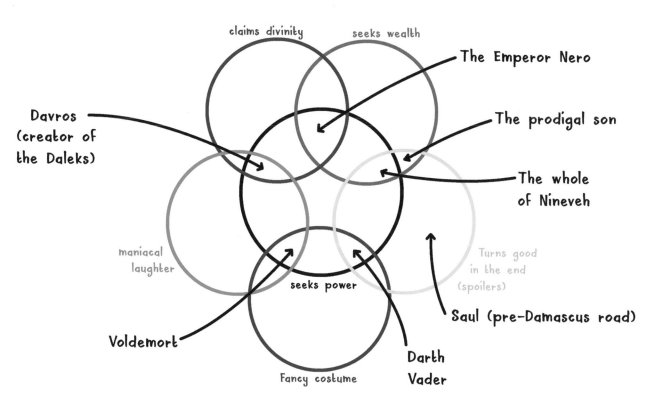

claims divinity

seeks wealth

The Emperor Nero

Davros (creator of the Daleks)

The prodigal son

The whole of Nineveh

maniacal laughter

seeks power

Turns good in the end (spoilers)

Saul (pre-Damascus road)

Voldemort

Fancy costume

Darth Vader

JESUS AND THE LAW

If you look back to the sect comparison website on page 55, I left a question mark over Jesus's attitude to the law of Torah (essentially, the first five books of the Old Testament). On the one hand, Jesus speaks of upholding the law, and even seems to intensify its demands. On the other hand, he seems opposed to any kind of legalism, and suggests that the whole law is summed up by the command to love. This is my interpretation of how to make sense of that, based on the idea that OT law is focussed on forming a people who love God faithfully, and love each other. The idea of this diagram is that the purpose is to build a house (representing love), and scaffolding (representing the law) is needed. With no scaffolding (antinomianism — lawlessness), the house is hard to build up because everyone's just doing whatever they choose, without regard to one another or God. But if the scaffolding becomes more important then the house never gets built.

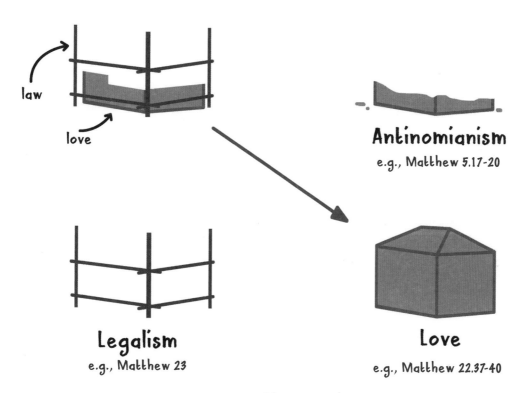

law

love

Antinomianism
e.g., Matthew 5.17-20

Legalism
e.g., Matthew 23

Love
e.g., Matthew 22.37-40

CONFLICT RESOLUTION

Being English, my instinctive approach to conflict is to not do it. This rarely does any good. In Matthew 18, Jesus suggests a more constructive approach to conflict, but also a more forgiving approach to each other than we might choose ourselves.

If nothing works in route (a), then Jesus suggests that the person is treated as an outsider (a gentile or tax-collector). This seems pretty harsh, but in the light of the whole of Matthew's account, it isn't unreasonable to ask how Jesus himself treats these so-called outsiders. Matthew 9.9-13 is just one example.

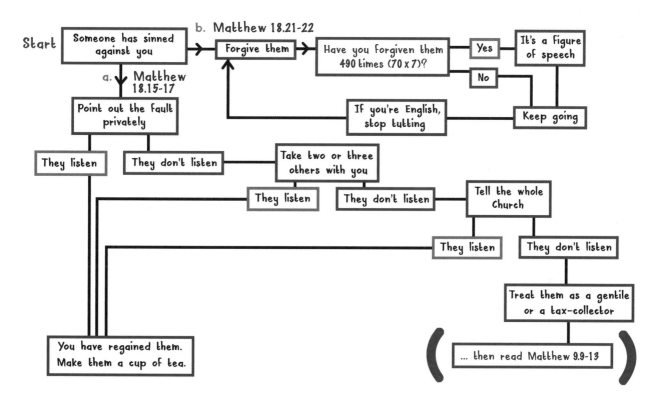

CAUSES OF WEEPING AND GNASHING OF TEETH

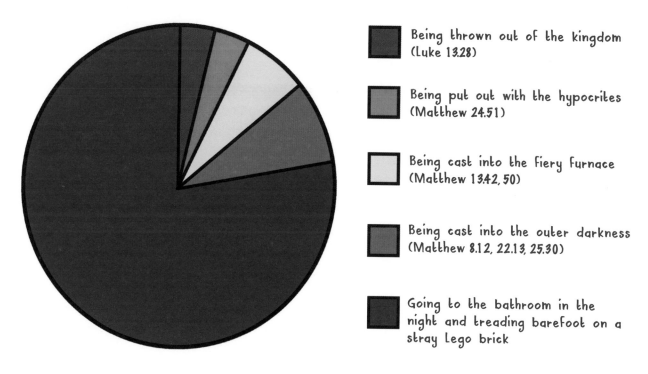

Being thrown out of the kingdom
(Luke 13.28)

Being put out with the hypocrites
(Matthew 24.51)

Being cast into the fiery furnace
(Matthew 13.42, 50)

Being cast into the outer darkness
(Matthew 8.12, 22.13, 25.30)

Going to the bathroom in the
night and treading barefoot on a
stray Lego brick

PASSION PREDICTIONS IN MARK

As we approach the climax of Mark's gospel, there's a repeated pattern through which we learn about Jesus's coming execution, and how that event should shape the way that the disciples live. I've reduced the content of these verses down just to illustrate what's going on, but more than ever it's worth reading the passages to see how the theme is developed.

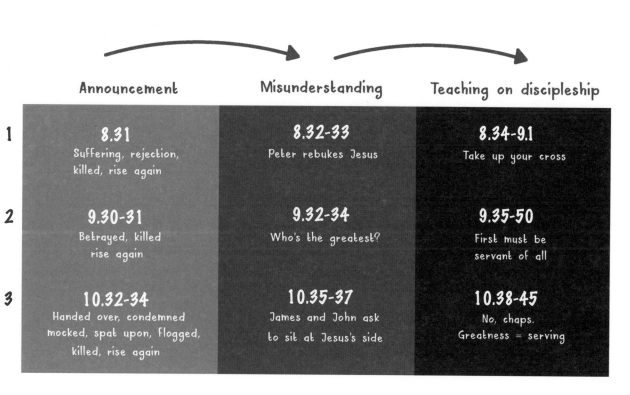

	Announcement	Misunderstanding	Teaching on discipleship
1	**8.31** Suffering, rejection, killed, rise again	**8.32-33** Peter rebukes Jesus	**8.34-9.1** Take up your cross
2	**9.30-31** Betrayed, killed rise again	**9.32-34** Who's the greatest?	**9.35-50** First must be servant of all
3	**10.32-34** Handed over, condemned mocked, spat upon, flogged, killed, rise again	**10.35-37** James and John ask to sit at Jesus's side	**10.38-45** No, chaps. Greatness = serving

JESUS THE REFUGEE

I'm going to close this chapter by returning to an early point in Jesus's life when his family have to flee Herod and escape to Egypt (Matthew 2.13-15), and taking account of two other themes (Matthew 8.20, and Mark 8.31 among others). It's quite familiar for Christians to ask the question 'What Would Jesus Do?', if he were around today. That's not a bad question to ask, but we should remember that Jesus's options were not necessarily the same as ours because of who and where he was. So perhaps the first question might be 'Who Would Jesus Be?' if he were around today.

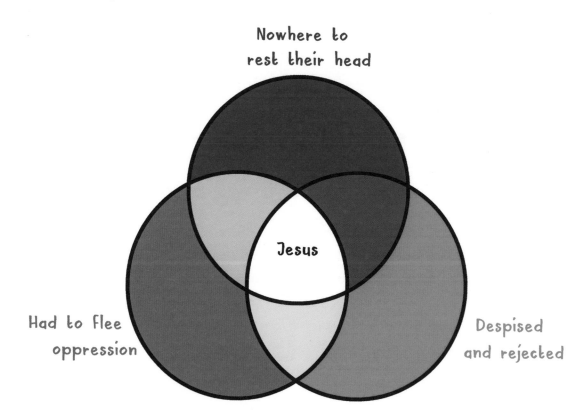

4

IN WHICH WE TRY TO MAKE SENSE OF WHAT JESUS HAS DONE

I suppose in reality this whole book is about trying to make sense of what Jesus has done, but in this section I'm really focusing on two things. One is how theology has reflected on the nature and significance of Jesus in ways that take us beyond his immediate context. The other concerns how we make sense of making sense, which I grant you is a sentence that's hard to make sense of. What I'm talking about here are the various ways that we think about how to understand theology, Jesus and the Bible. This will involve developing a bit of what we've already talked about on the subject of interpretation and things. To be honest, its probably better if we just crack on with it.

THE ATONEMENT

How is it that Jesus reconciles humanity with God? People often describe three ways of thinking about it, though there are probably more variations on each theme. Anselm became Archbishop of Canterbury in 1093 and argued that humanity must pay for its sin but that the cost is so great that only God can meet it. Jesus, as God and human, offers a once and for all sacrifice from us to God to deal with sin. Peter Abelard (1079-1142) was a French theologian generally credited with suggesting that God redeems humanity by transforming us. Jesus's sacrifice demonstrates God's love and inspires us to love alike. Gustaf Aulén was a modern theologian but he argued that before those guys came along, the earliest Christians primarily saw Jesus as defeating evil, the devil and death, all the things holding humanity captive. Sadly I've run out of space to tell you who's correct. Could be all three.

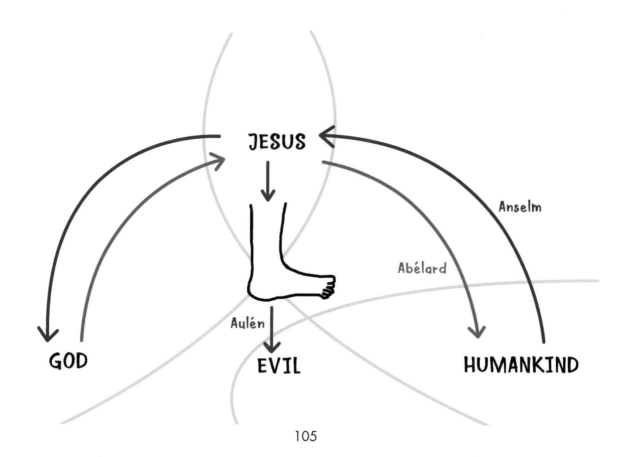

JESUS

GOD

EVIL

HUMANKIND

Anselm

Abélard

Aulén

105

JOY

Luke 15.7

I don't know why but I find the word atonement slightly scary, so let's move on to joy.

Quantity of joy

99 righteous persons

One sinner that repents

Hearing that one's children are walking in truth (3 John 4)

Finding ten pounds in your pocket that you'd forgotten about

Finding ten pounds in your pocket after it's been through the wash (p.s. The UK is about to launch a £10 note that can survive a washing machine, so this diagram has already dated. Many apologies.)

THE WORD OF GOD (1)
Hebrews 4.12

I have two dogs, one of whom is a Patterdale terrier. He quite often gets distracted on walks and plunges headfirst into either the other dog or my shins. Active yes, but not the sharpest of canine minds.

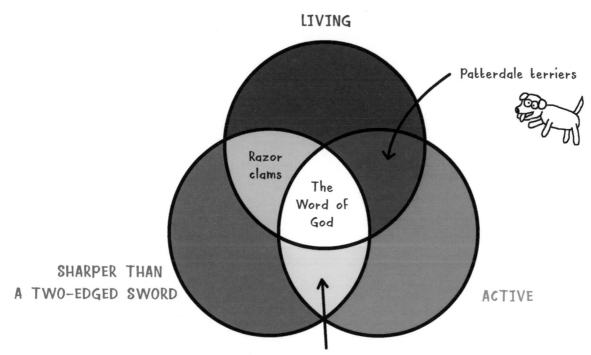

LIVING

Patterdale terriers

Razor clams

The Word of God

SHARPER THAN
A TWO-EDGED SWORD

ACTIVE

The sword guarding Eden
(Genesis 3.24)

THE WORD OF GOD (2)

But what is the word of God? The Bible contains a number of references to the word of God covering a range of possibilities, but people also speak about the Bible itself as the word of God. And then of course, Jesus is described as the word in John chapter 1. This diagram is partially based on the Swiss theologian Karl Barth (1886-1968), though without explanation I could get into some serious trouble.

The point of this is not to say, for example, that some parts of scripture are the word of God and some aren't. The idea is that the Word of God refers to God's revelation to us, and for Christians that is Jesus. Barth said that the Bible becomes the word of God in its revealing Jesus to us. Similarly, when preaching becomes the occasion for Jesus being made known, it can be described as a moment of preaching the word of God. Of course there are other views.

Jesus Christ

The Word of God

Human words

Scripture

Preaching

THE FOURFOLD SENSE OF SCRIPTURE

Sometimes people speak of the Medieval fourfold sense of scripture, though that probably doesn't do justice to a thousand ish years of Medieval interpretation. But these four senses remain part of the Catholic Church's teaching today, and reflect the long-standing idea that God can speak through scripture on multiple levels. The literal level remains primary, but literal here doesn't mean literalistic, so the literal sense might also be allegorical if that's what the genre of the text indicates. 'Tropological' refers to a moral sense of meaning, and 'anagogical' refers to the text lifting our minds to the heavenly future.

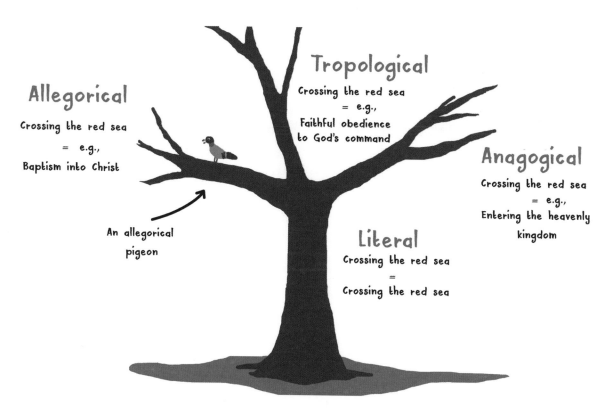

Allegorical

Crossing the red sea
= e.g.,
Baptism into Christ

Tropological

Crossing the red sea
= e.g.,
Faithful obedience
to God's command

Anagogical

Crossing the red sea
= e.g.,
Entering the heavenly
kingdom

Literal

Crossing the red sea
=
Crossing the red sea

An allegorical
pigeon

CHIASMS

I mentioned earlier that Fido's breakfast forms a chiasm (page 82). What is a chiasm you say? Well, it's a literary device that draws your attention to a particular focus by following a kind of symmetrical shape. Whatever is at the middle becomes the defining moment. The technique is named after the Greek letter chi (grey in the background here), which like an X draws the attention into the centre.

a. Meeting someone you can't quite place

A. Awkward recognition, but can't remember who it is

B. Opening pleasantries

C. Chatting cautiously, asking questions to work out who it is

D. Realisation of who it is / moment it's polite to wrap it up

C'. Chatting confidently, like you knew all along

B'. Closing pleasantries

A'. Awkward exit, did I get away with it?

b. Luke 24

A. Journey: Jerusalem – Emmaus (v13)

B. Jesus appears, eyes kept from recognising him (vv15-16)

C. Talk, questions (vv17-18)

D. Disciples tell story of Jesus (vv19-21)

E. Empty tomb, vision of angels (vv22-23)

F. Jesus is proclaimed to be alive (v23)

E'. Empty tomb, no sight of Jesus (v24)

D'. Jesus explains his story from scripture (vv25-27)

C'. Talk, breaking of bread (vv28-30)

B'. Eyes opened to recognise Jesus, Jesus disappears (v31)

A'. Return journey: Emmaus – Jerusalem (vv33-35)

SOME CREEDS

Some folks will be very familiar with these creeds (though possibly less the Athanasian creed), while others may not be. They have quite complex histories but represent statements of faith used in many Churches (again, probably less the Athanasian creed) based on the accumulation of thought and wisdom over time. Here we can see some common points, and the differences need not be contradictory, but instead reflect different emphases.

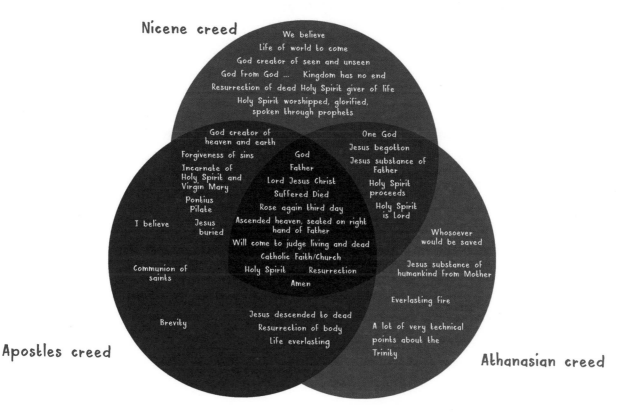

Nicene creed

We believe
Life of world to come
God creator of seen and unseen
God from God ...   Kingdom has no end
Resurrection of dead Holy Spirit giver of life
Holy Spirit worshipped, glorified,
spoken through prophets

God creator of
heaven and earth
Forgiveness of sins
Incarnate of
Holy Spirit and
Virgin Mary
Pontius
Pilate

God
Father
Lord Jesus Christ
Suffered Died
Rose again third day
Ascended heaven, seated on right
hand of Father
Will come to judge living and dead
Catholic Faith/Church
Holy Spirit   Resurrection
Amen

One God
Jesus begotton
Jesus substance of
Father
Holy Spirit
proceeds
Holy Spirit
is Lord

I believe   Jesus
buried

Whosoever
would be saved

Communion of
saints

Jesus substance of
humankind from Mother

Everlasting fire

Brevity

Jesus descended to dead
Resurrection of body
Life everlasting

A lot of very technical
points about the
Trinity

Apostles creed

Athanasian creed

117

HEAVENLY ASCENT

In 2 Corinthians 12.2, Paul refers to someone (probably himself) being caught up into the third heaven. WHAT DOES THAT MEAN? I hear you ask. Well we don't know, but this is one of those things that probably made a lot more sense at the time. What we do know is that lots of other writings from that time and beyond speak of ascending through various levels of heaven. Some talk about three levels, others five, and quite a lot talk of seven. Which is where we get the phrase seventh heaven. So is Paul saying he made it all the way to the top of a three-tier heaven (A), or only as far as level three in a seven-tier heaven (B)? The best way to answer that is to look at what else is going on in that part of 2 Corinthians. But most people manage to live happily without ever wondering.

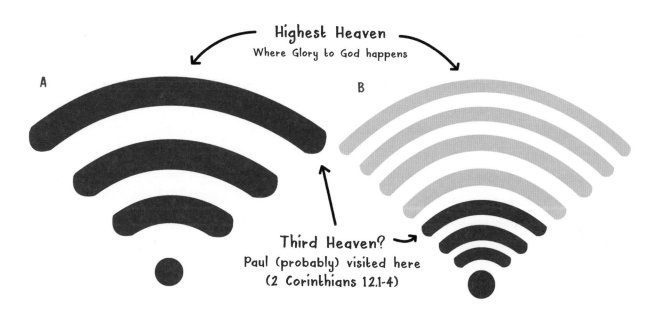

Highest Heaven
Where Glory to God happens

A

B

Third Heaven?
Paul (probably) visited here
(2 Corinthians 12.1-4)

THE ESCALATOR (?) OF SALVATION

Keeping with the theme of ascending, though mostly because I drew an escalator, this diagram ponders the nature of salvation. In particular, the New Testament is able to talk about salvation as something that has happened, something that we are in the midst of, and something that is in the future. I suppose my suggestion is that all three dimensions are important to consider. I'm not sure if the escalator adds much to this point, though it might just suggest that salvation is a work of God (rather than a human effort), while remaining open to stuff about running the race ahead of us (e.g., Hebrews 12.1). Though obviously don't run on a real escalator.

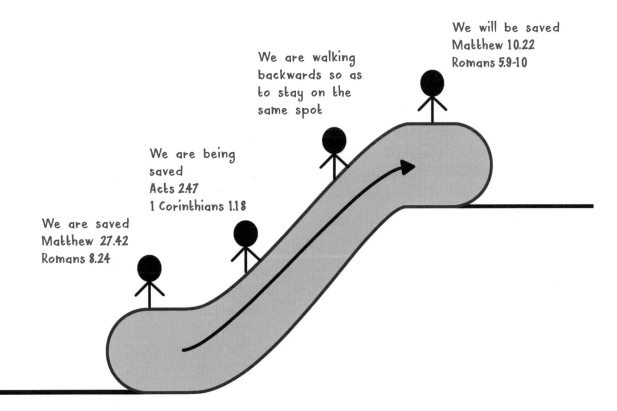

We will be saved
Matthew 10.22
Romans 5.9-10

We are walking
backwards so as
to stay on the
same spot

We are being
saved
Acts 2.47
1 Corinthians 1.18

We are saved
Matthew 27.42
Romans 8.24

AUTHORS, TEXTS, AND READERS

When we read a text in the Bible, how do we figure out what it means? A fair start is to say it means whatever the *author* intended it to mean, but if the author lived 2000 years ago then it's impossible to check. So maybe it's the *text* that really matters, and indeed legal documents are often carefully worded so that the text's meaning is 100% clear. But even legal texts still have to be interpreted, and if scripture is meant to change us, perhaps what really matters is whatever the text means to the *reader* in that moment. Bible study groups often discuss what the text says to each person then and there. But in that way, no reader is isolated, and so the *communities* that shape them will also shape what the text means to them. Indeed, authors and readers often share a sort of community even if they're separated by many years.

So no answers here, but lots to think about.

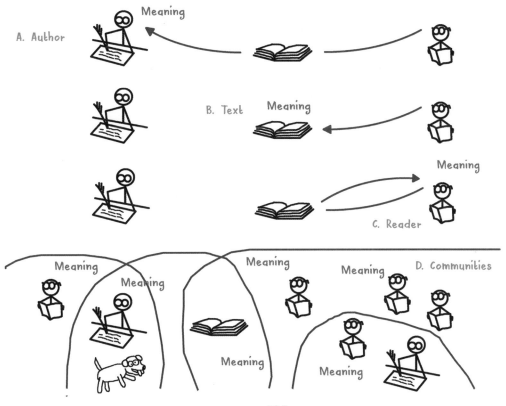

A. Author

Meaning

B. Text

Meaning

C. Reader

Meaning

D. Communities

Meaning

Meaning

Meaning

Meaning

Meaning

Meaning

LINGUISTIC COMMUNITIES

I mentioned on the last page the idea that our communities form what things mean to us. So what you think of when you see the word 'pain' depends on whether you were formed in a French or English speaking community ('pain' being French for bread if I remember rightly). In the same way, working out what 'a manger' means depends on working out whether you're in Church at Christmas, or in London looking for a sandwich. A lot of people inhabit both communities, so easily work out the difference. This might seem like an incredibly obvious point, but consider the word 'heart'. We tend to associate the heart with emotions, distinct from the head where thinking happens. But is that what the communities from which biblical texts spring thought it meant? In the Bible, the heart probably includes emotions and thoughts, and so it can help to try and check how our preconceptions about meaning influence the way we read scripture.

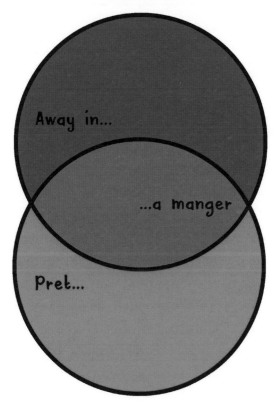

Away in...

...a manger

Pret...

WORDS AND ACTIONS

They say actions speak louder than words, but words can be powerful (and not just in a magical, *expecto patronum* kind of a way). All of the statements along the top here could just be passing along information, and so won't need much response. But normally they actually do something that changes the world, getting a stronger response. Saying 'I love you' is an act of love; when the referee says 'offside', that verdict changes the game; when I make a promise, expectations are raised that aren't easily unraised without cost. And religious language like 'I believe', 'I repent' or 'I confess' can do more than just let God know what we're thinking; such words can be spiritual acts, and they can change us as well. Philosophers call this 'speech act theory', and a strong speech act makes some kind of difference in the world.

	"I love you"	"Offside!"	"I promise to put the bins out"	"I repent"
Response if it's a plain statement	How interesting, thanks for letting me know	How interesting, thanks for letting me know	How interesting, thanks for letting me know	How interesting, thanks for letting me know
Response if it's a strong speech act	I love you too	WHAT!?!?!?! You must be joking That was never offside! etc etc	Much weeping and gnashing of teeth as I once again forget to put the bins out	Rejoicing in heaven

DIFFERENT HOPES

People will often talk about hope in different ways depending on what their hope is based on. Modern optimism saw the possibility of gradual progress, without saying where it would lead. Some followers of Marx (and others) believe that a sort of perfect utopian future is possible within history, though with a rocky road to get there. Apocalyptic hope, expressed by Jesus in Mark 13, or in Revelation (and lots of other places) can look gloomy until a decisive moment where things are turned around by an act of God. What does Christian hope look like? All of these have featured in the history of theology.

1. Optimistic

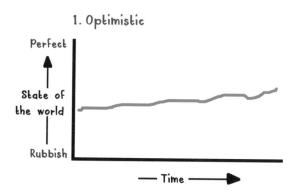

2. Utopian

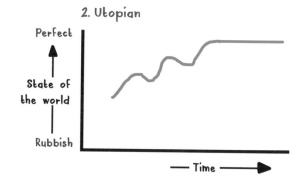

3. Apocalyptic

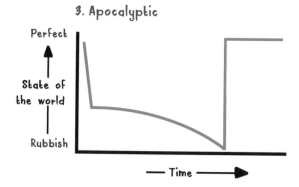

4. According to the Daily Mule

'First century Galilee's most popular daily paper'

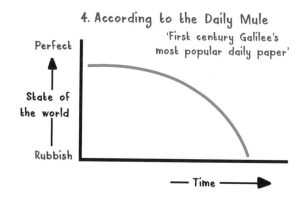

THE TROUSERS OF HOPE

I'm a big fan of pondering apparent paradoxes in the Bible, and this one has to do with hope and judgement. Some passages are dualistic, meaning that the good and the evil will be judged and sent their separate ways. Other passages are universalistic, meaning that all creation gets redeemed. What this diagram suggests is that this tension is important, if the metaphorical trousers of hope are to stay up. Dualism points to a God who takes evil seriously, and who cares about justice. Universalism points to a God whose goodness is without limit, whose love cannot be overcome. People will resolve this tension in different ways, but all I'm suggesting is that the tension arises from seeking to affirm important things about God. Using only one brace may prove uncomfortable.

Universalism
e.g., Revelation 21.5

Dualism
e.g., Matthew 25

A REVELATION INFOGRAPHIC

After drawing this it occurred to me that it's missing at least one really vital theme from Revelation, that being the heavenly visions and the visions of Christ (broadly chapters 1, 4-5, 21-22). Anyway, the plan was that because Revelation is such a visual book, it might be interesting to visualize the whole thing a glance. On that basis, this diagram shows some images which create structure, some that are key themes, and the four horses of the apocalypse (in chapter 6).

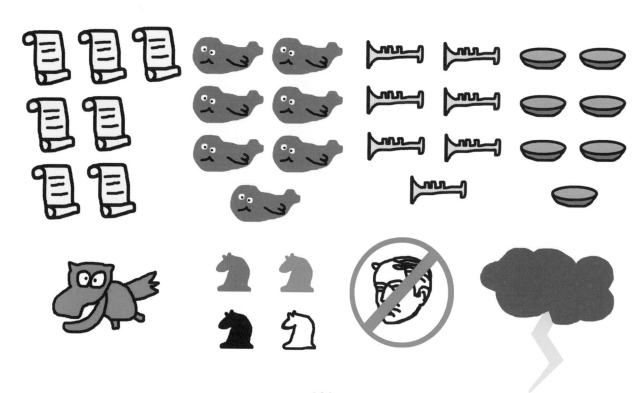

HEAVEN AND EARTH COMING TOGETHER

We already had a think about heaven earlier, and it's quite a mystery. Sometimes we think of Christian hope as being about going to heaven when we die; that may not be wrong, but the Bible has more to say, and sometimes describes heaven coming to earth and somehow being joined together. If that's right, we could think of that beginning with the coming of Jesus. And whatever heaven and earth coming together means, it suggests that the Christian hope is for more, not less, than what we experience now. Therefore, less of the playing harps on a cloud type stuff.

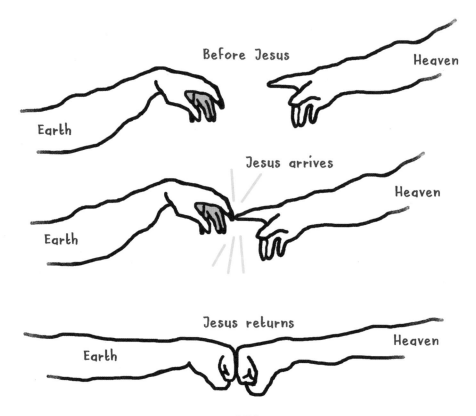

5

IN WHICH WE TRY TO LIVE FAITHFULLY. OR SOMETHING.

A bit of me wants to introduce this chapter as the collection of miscellaneous leftovers, but that doesn't sound very impressive so I won't do that. I think what connects this last collection is that they illustrate things to do with the ways of life that have been formed through taking Christian faith and theology on board. So some of it's to do with the Church, some to do with ethics, and some to do with prayer and worship. Also, predictably, some of it is just miscellaneous leftovers.

THE HOLY SPIRIT

This diagram only dips our toes into the waters of what we could say about the Holy Spirit, but it compares two lists in Paul's letters that describe the work of the Holy Spirit in communities (Galatians 5 on fruits and 1 Corinthians 12-14 on gifts). In particular, while some of the more exciting gifts often get a lot of attention in Churches, it's faith (or faithfulness) that links both passages.

And who doesn't like to receive dried fruit?

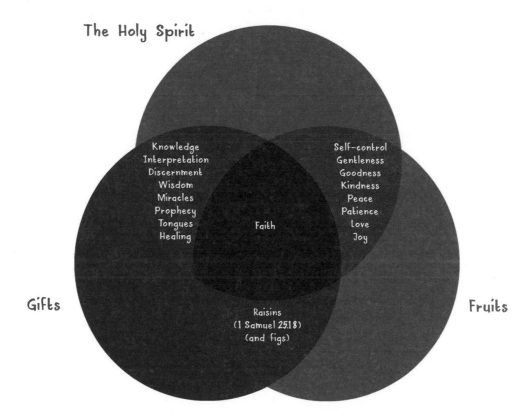

The Holy Spirit

Knowledge
Interpretation
Discernment
Wisdom
Miracles
Prophecy
Tongues
Healing

Self-control
Gentleness
Goodness
Kindness
Peace
Patience
Love
Joy

Faith

Gifts

Fruits

Raisins
(1 Samuel 25.18)
(and figs)

THE CHURCH'S YEAR

For a long time now the Church has, in various ways, remembered the life of Jesus by structuring its worship through the year to tell Christ's story. In some traditions different colours mark out the different seasons. In the commercial world, the year is structured through sugary treats and they tend to appear a little ahead of the Church calendar.

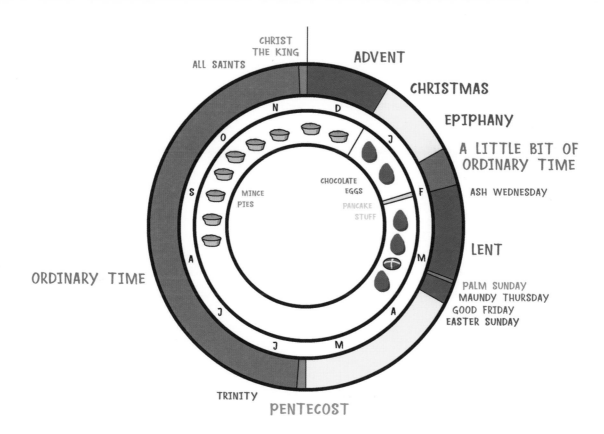

CHRIST THE KING

ALL SAINTS

ADVENT

CHRISTMAS

EPIPHANY

A LITTLE BIT OF ORDINARY TIME

ASH WEDNESDAY

LENT

PALM SUNDAY
MAUNDY THURSDAY
GOOD FRIDAY
EASTER SUNDAY

ORDINARY TIME

TRINITY

PENTECOST

MINCE PIES

CHOCOLATE EGGS

PANCAKE STUFF

N D J F M A M J J A S O

WHAT IS BAPTISM?

The more I think about it, the less sure I am. But here are some (hopefully) relevant thoughts. The bits below the font are ideas and practices that might be like precursors to Christian baptism; for example we mentioned the Essenes earlier on page 55. They did a lot of ritual washing. The bits in purple are to do with where baptism might come in the life of faith. The bits at the top are to do with the relationship between water and spirit, human acts and God's grace, and the symbolism of dying and rising in Christ.

And now that I've said all that, the diagram is a bit redundant.

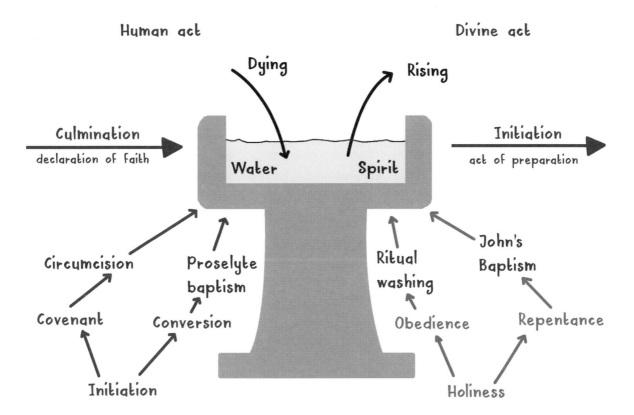

Human act

Divine act

Dying

Rising

Culmination
declaration of faith

Initiation
act of preparation

Water

Spirit

Circumcision

Proselyte
baptism

Ritual
washing

John's
Baptism

Covenant

Conversion

Obedience

Repentance

Initiation

Holiness

PRAYER

Prayer is a funny thing; Christians have always done it, but often wondered what 'it' actually was. In particular, if God knows everything, and God's will is for what is best, then why do we need to ask for things? This diagram suggests one answer; God wants what is best for the world, but what is best for the world includes humans wanting what is best for the world too, and that can be expressed through prayer. Of course this isn't the only kind of prayer, as we shall see.

GOD

HUMANKIND
RESPONDS

PRAYER

GOD ENGAGES
HUMANKIND

HUMANKIND

A PRAYERNNEAGRAM

This diagram might look like a weird secret society symbol or something, but it is actually ripped off from the enneagram personality profile system. If you knew that already, that won't help as to be honest I just liked the way it looked. But here are some different ideas that you might associate with prayer, reflecting different kinds of emphases. The only tenuous link I can make with the enneagram is the possibility that we find ourselves more naturally drawn to some types of prayer than others, but (almost) all of these find expression in the Bible, and especially in the Psalms.

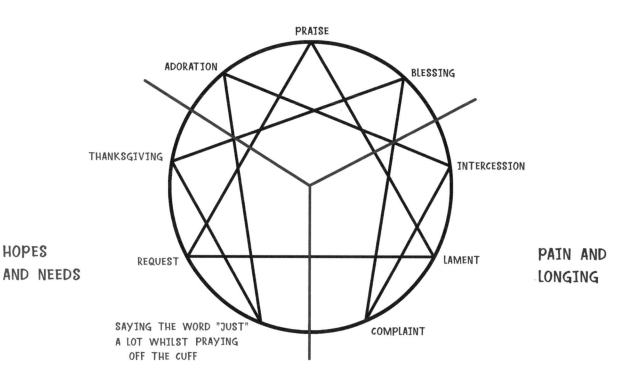

WORSHIP

PRAISE

ADORATION

BLESSING

THANKSGIVING

INTERCESSION

HOPES
AND NEEDS

PAIN AND
LONGING

REQUEST

LAMENT

SAYING THE WORD "JUST"
A LOT WHILST PRAYING
OFF THE CUFF

COMPLAINT

THE GOLDEN MEAN OF VIRTUE

Virtue ethics is a way of doing ethics that focuses on what kind of characteristics (virtues) make for a good person. This goes back to giants of Greek philosophy like Aristotle, and was picked up by Thomas Aquinas (1225-1274), a boss of the Medieval theological tradition known as scholasticism. Classically, virtues look for the 'golden mean' between two vices, one where the virtue is lacking, and one where it's gone a bit over the top.

Vice	Virtue	Vice 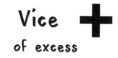
of deficiency		of excess

a. the virtue of moistness in a cake

Dry

Moist
Mary Berry is pleased

Soggy-bottomed

b. the virtue of fortitude in people

Cowardice

Fortitude

Foolhardiness
Mary Berry is not pleased

THEOLOGICAL VIRTUES

As well as describing the cardinal virtues of fortitude, prudence, temperance and justice, Thomas (Aquinas) also described three theological virtues, namely faith, hope, and love. But while the other virtues find a mid-point between too little or too much of a good thing, Thomas thought that it didn't make sense to say that you could love (for example) too much. So in a sense, the theological virtues work in three dimensions; they still have corresponding pitfalls (vices if you will), but they can also grow and grow in a Godly sense. So here, you can't have too much hope in God, yet there are dangers of falling into despair on the one hand, or presumptuousness on the other.

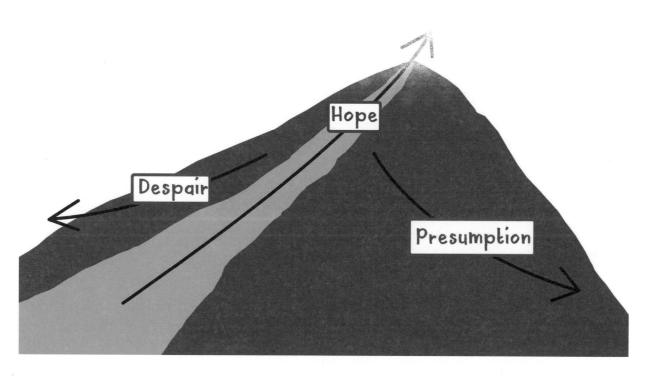

THESE THINGS ENDURE
1 Corinthians 13.13

This might be one place from which Thomas (Aquinas) got the idea for three theological virtues. St Paul describes these things as enduring to the very end and beyond.

Now these things endure

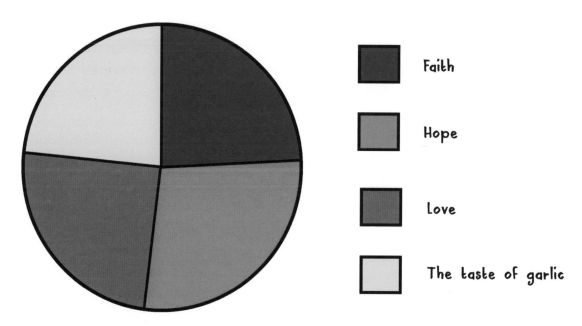

Faith

Hope

Love

The taste of garlic

GROWING IN WISDOM
1 Corinthians 13.11

P.S. I know this isn't really what pie charts are for, so apologies to any mathematical purists out there.

When I was a child ...

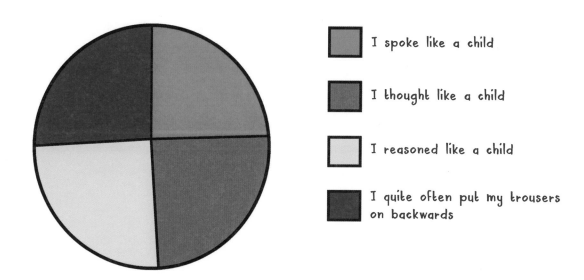

I spoke like a child

I thought like a child

I reasoned like a child

I quite often put my trousers on backwards

WHAT'S WHAT IN A CHURCH BUILDING

This is what might be described as a 'classic' of Church architecture, though not all Church buildings look like this by any means. I grew up going to a Church that was converted from an early cinema, and had kept the cinema seats, so I've never understood why on earth anyone would choose to install pews. Except that pews are quieter when everyone stands up.

NORTH
MAYBE AN ORGAN OR SOMETHING?
TRANSEPT

TOYS FOR CHILDREN
KETTLE, COFFEE
BISCUITS, OLD BOOKS

N O R T H   A I S L E
FONT?

FONT?
MAYBE THE
ORGAN COULD
BE HERE

UNEVEN FLOOR

A PRETTY WINDOW
WEST END
POSH CHURCHES HAVE AN
EXTRA BIT OF ORGAN HERE

MINI
BAR

PULPIT/
LECTERN

AUMBRY

CHOIR

EAST END
HIGH ALTAR

NAVE

PEWS PEWS P
E
W
S
PEWS

PEWS

CROSSING

STEPS (MAYBE)
(OR A ROOD SCREEN)

QUIRE

TABLE

PEWS PEWS PEWS

FONT?

SERVICE
BOOKS

SOUTH AISLE

MAYBE
SOME
LITTLE
CANDLES

LECTERN /
PULPIT

CHOIR

PORCH
LOST UMBRELLAS

F O N T ?

HEATER

SOUTH
TRANSEPT
MORE WINDOWS PROBABLY
(AND OBVIOUSLY A WALL)

KEEPING THE PEACE

The letter to Titus offers some suggestions for things to avoid if we want a harmonious existence. Given that Matthew's gospel starts with a genealogy, I hope there won't be an embarrassing silence when Paul (named as the writer to Titus) and Matthew meet in the heavenly kingdom, and Matthew asks Paul why he told everyone to avoid genealogies. (see page 41).

Mind you, Peter says that some things in Paul's letters are 'hard to understand' (2 Peter 3.16), so if Matthew says anything awkward about Peter, we've got a nice triangle going of controversy going on there. I'm not going to put that in a diagram though.

Things to avoid

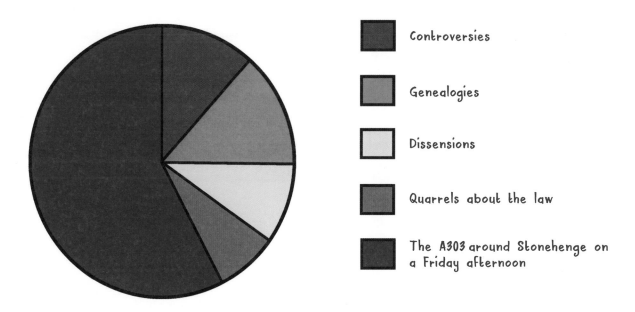

- Controversies
- Genealogies
- Dissensions
- Quarrels about the law
- The A303 around Stonehenge on a Friday afternoon

TRICKY CHARACTERS

Although if I did, it would look something like this. This is a bit silly but the reason I put this in is that I hope it brings out the lively dynamics of the first Christians. When the letter to Titus talks about avoiding genealogies, I think it's talking about unnecessary debates or rivalries about who is the most noble, so there's no actual conflict with Matthew or Luke's genealogies of Jesus. But if this diagram helps, I hope it's by highlighting the way the New Testament writers don't try and hide away the complexities of the real life of faith in community.

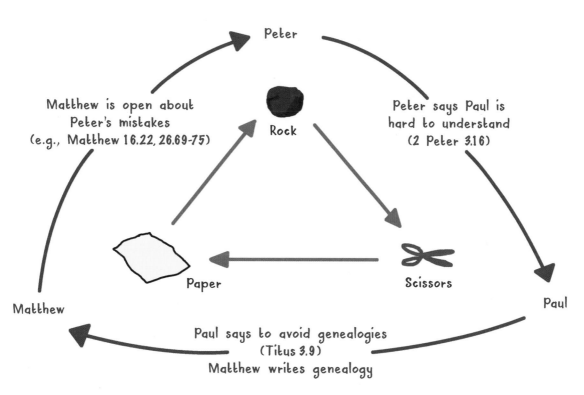

Peter

Matthew is open about
Peter's mistakes
(e.g., Matthew 16.22, 26.69-75)

Rock

Peter says Paul is
hard to understand
(2 Peter 3.16)

Paper

Scissors

Matthew

Paul

Paul says to avoid genealogies
(Titus 3.9)
Matthew writes genealogy

MAKING SENSE OF MONOTHEISM

Monotheism — believing in one God — might seem like a simple idea, but early on, Romans called Christians atheists because the Christians denied all the Roman gods. In our day, some atheists argue the same way, saying that if Christians deny all those other gods, then why not let go of one more? But what does 'god' actually mean?

We might think of monotheism as saying that there's this thing called a god, and we think there's only one of them (that's diagram 3.). But when the first commandment says 'you shall have no other gods before me', the emphasis seems to fall on relationship. Existence or non-existence of other beings is not the issue; what matters is that YHWH (see page 14) is the only god for them. Here, believing in one god has more to do with saying that there's only one being that they worship and follow. That's diagram 4. It's not an either or thing, but suggests that there may be different biblical dimensions to believing in one god.

1. Atheism

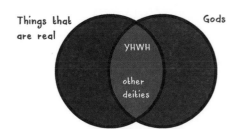

2. Polytheism

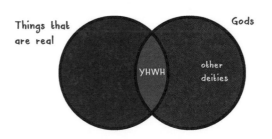

3. Monotheism (a)

4. Monotheism (b)

ADVENT

Traditionally, Advent is the season of preparation for celebrating the coming of Christ at Christmas, and so also for thinking about the coming of Christ in the hope of resurrection, judgement and renewal. The four weeks leading up to Christmas are marked with candles, and various ways of reflecting on the Christian story. Or anything in groups of four.

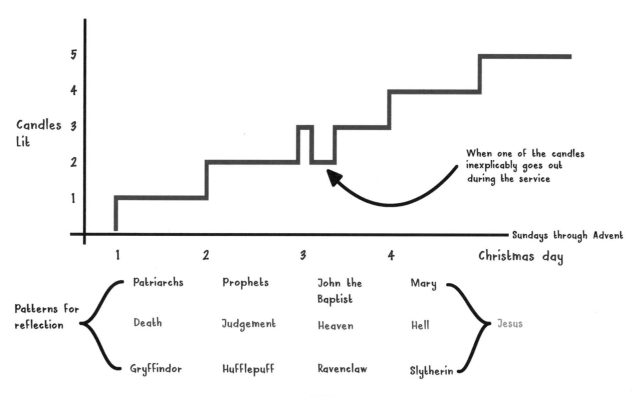

Candles Lit

5
4
3
2
1

Sundays through Advent

1   2   3   4   Christmas day

When one of the candles inexplicably goes out during the service

Patterns for reflection

Patriarchs	Prophets	John the Baptist	Mary	
Death	Judgement	Heaven	Hell	Jesus
Gryffindor	Hufflepuff	Ravenclaw	Slytherin	

THE PROSPERITY GOSPEL

I generally try to avoid expressing too many strong opinions, but there's quite a big movement in the Church these days that suggests that if you have enough faith, you will be wealthy and prosperous and probably have a private jet. This is my analysis of that view.

Problems with the prosperity gospel

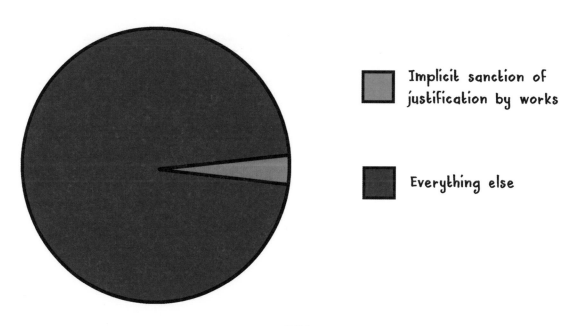

- Implicit sanction of justification by works
- Everything else

THE PRECEPTS OF NATURAL LAW

The idea of the natural law is that you can rationally work out how to live, based on our created nature. It begins with suggesting that it is rational to pursue whatever is good. Thomas Aquinas (him again) developed a version of this theory, and it is generally said that he names five primary precepts that guide natural law thinking. These five then guide us onto secondary precepts that relate to specific scenarios. When he describes these five precepts in his *Summa Theologiae*, he actually leaves room for more, and I've taken advantage of that room.

Primary Precepts

Secondary Precepts

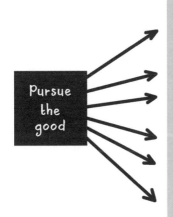

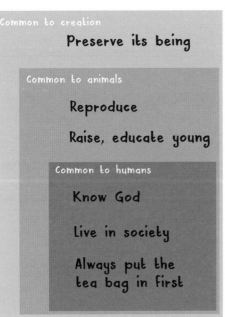

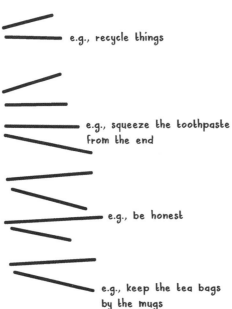

Common to creation

Preserve its being

e.g., recycle things

Common to animals

Reproduce

Raise, educate young

e.g., squeeze the toothpaste from the end

Common to humans

Know God

Live in society

Always put the tea bag in first

e.g., be honest

e.g., keep the tea bags by the mugs

Pursue the good

THE ARMOUR OF GOD

Around the time the letter to the Ephesians was written, the Roman soldier was a fearsome presence across the known world. Probably more so than this guy. But the military armour is taken up in Ephesians chapter 6 as a metaphor for the ways in which God protects people through the trials of life, especially when the world is hostile to faith. However, these images also draw on texts that go back before Roman times. They connect this passage with similar ideas expressed in the Old Testament, suggesting a sense of God's ongoing protection over a longer history.

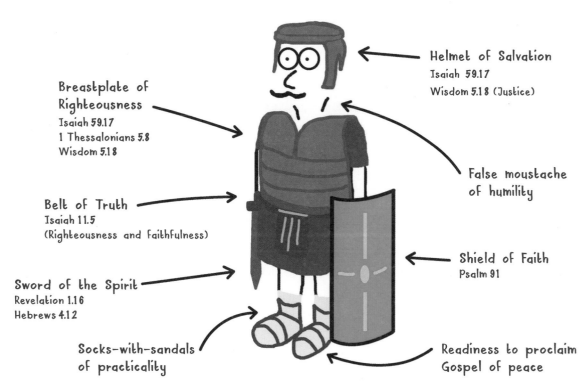

Helmet of Salvation
Isaiah 59.17
Wisdom 5.18 (Justice)

Breastplate of
Righteousness
Isaiah 59.17
1 Thessalonians 5.8
Wisdom 5.18

False moustache
of humility

Belt of Truth
Isaiah 11.5
(Righteousness and faithfulness)

Shield of Faith
Psalm 91

Sword of the Spirit
Revelation 1.16
Hebrews 4.12

Socks-with-sandals
of practicality

Readiness to proclaim
Gospel of peace

CONCLUSION

I can't decide whether at the end of a book you should feel more or less knowledgeable. On the one hand, it seems obvious that I should want you to close the book with a satisfied sense of having gained much information, but on the other hand much of what we've looked at here reminds us of the complexity of talking about God. So while it may be just me, I've often found that as I learn I become more aware of what I don't understand. Which kind of takes us back to the beginning, with faith still seeking understanding, and maybe that's ok.

What I would say (and thanks by the way if you made all the way to end with me), is that I'd encourage you to notice if any of the diagrams sparked your interest, and look into those themes in more depth. It may mean reading an unfamiliar part of the Bible, exploring some of the authors mentioned, or talking with others. And perhaps praying. Whatever you take away from the book, remember this; giraffes understand everything.

And as I say farewell, here's one final diagram.

PSALM 23

Psalm 23 is probably one of the most popular Psalms and perhaps one of the best-known bits of the Bible. And, as we were thinking about complexity in the conclusion, it serves as a good reminder that in the midst of all that, it is still meaningful to say some simple but profound things about God. And life.

Things that will follow me all the days of my life

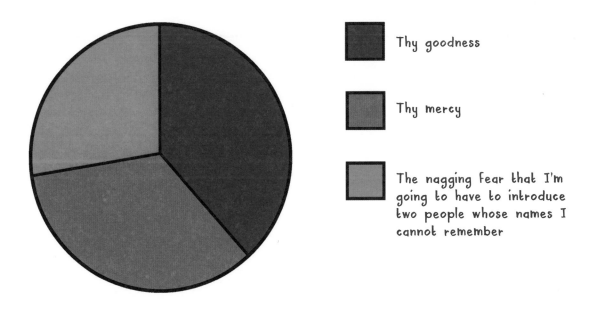

- Thy goodness
- Thy mercy
- The nagging fear that I'm going to have to introduce two people whose names I cannot remember